MW00883448

THIS BOOK BELONGS TO:

INTRODUCTION

WELCOME TO THE OFFICE SURVIVAL GUIDE

Welcome to the Office Survival Guide, your new best friend in the world of workplace "productivity." This isn't your typical guide to climbing the corporate ladder or unlocking your full potential—nope, we're here to teach you the real secret to success: the art of looking busy.

OVERVIEW OF THE "FAKE IT 'TIL YOU MAKE IT" PHILOSOPHY

There are superstars at every company, those people who never give up and are always one step ahead. On the other hand, there are those of us who are only attempting to get through each day without becoming distracted by mindless thoughts about food or playing cat videos.

If you're the kind of hero who knows that, sometimes, it's more fun to pretend to be productive than to really get anything done, then this guide is for you. The "Fake It 'Til You Make It" mentality is fully supported here. In this course, you will learn the subtle techniques that will allow you to project an image of productivity even when you aren't actively working out. Why work hard when you can look like you're working?

KEY TENETS OF THE "FAKE IT 'TIL YOU MAKE IT" PHILOSOPHY

- **Master the Look:** Just like a magician keeps you guessing, you'll charm your coworkers and boss into not noticing that you're a bit lost. Master the furrowed brow, the "thinking pose," and the "I'm just wrapping up something important" look.
- **Embrace the Excitement of Buzzwords:** You don't have to fully grasp ideas like "synergy" or "optimization." Just sprinkle them into your chats and emails, and see how people nod along, thinking you've got everything under control.
- **The Busy Desk Illusion:** A cluttered desk sure seems like a busy desk, doesn't it? Just scatter some sticky notes here and there, set an open binder on one side, and there you have it! Immediate trustworthiness.
- **The Art of "In Progress":** It's best to avoid saying you're finished with something, as that tends to invite more work. Instead, it's always "a work in progress." This enchanting phrase gives you a moment to breathe and shows your careful commitment.

A FEW WORDS OF ENCOURAGEMENT

Just keep in mind, "Fake It 'Til You Make It" is a skill that many office workers have mastered over the years. You're in good company on this journey.

Whether you're skillfully avoiding meetings, appearing deeply focused on a "project," or crafting the ideal vague email response, remember that you're part of a wonderful tradition of employees who look busy and engaged.

This book is designed to be your helpful guide, your supportive mentor, and your best friend in the journey to appear like the busiest person in the office without any effort at all. In the corporate world, perception often shapes reality.

Now, grab your coffee, strike your best "thoughtful" pose, and let's have some fun!

GUIDE TO OFFICE SLANG

Ah, office slang—the fun little phrases that help you feel in the loop, even when you're not quite sure what's going on. Getting a good handle on these buzzwords is important in any workplace, where just sounding productive can sometimes be seen as more valuable than actually being productive. Here's a helpful glossary of some of the most commonly used (and often misunderstood) office buzzwords. Drop them into your chats and see your coworkers nod in agreement, totally impressed by your insight.

OFFICE BUZZWORD GLOSSARY

Synergy

- Definition: When two or more things work together to create something greater than they could alone (or at least that's the idea). Usage Tip: Works in almost any context where teamwork is involved, e.g., "Let's leverage our synergy on this project." Bonus points if you can say it with a straight face.

Leverage

- Definition: Fancy word for "use" that implies strategic brilliance. Usage Tip: Replace "use" with "leverage" to instantly sound like you have a game plan. Example: "We need to leverage our existing resources."

Circle Back

- Definition: Checking in or following up on something later (usually after everyone's forgotten about it). Usage Tip: Use it to avoid giving an answer. "Let's circle back to that next week."

Bandwidth

- Definition: Your capacity to handle tasks; derived from the world of internet speeds. Usage Tip: Claim to have "limited bandwidth" to dodge extra work. Example: "I'd love to, but I don't have the bandwidth for it right now."

Touch Base

- Definition: A quick check-in or meeting to discuss something. Usage Tip: Usually suggested when you're not really sure what to do next. "Let's touch base later to go over our progress."

Deep Dive
- Definition: An in-depth analysis, often into something no one cares about. Usage Tip: Suggest a "deep dive" to impress people with your commitment to "understanding the details." Example: "Maybe we should do a deep dive into last quarter's data."

Alignment
- Definition: Ensuring everyone is on the same page, even if no one actually knows what the page is. Usage Tip: Great for making it sound like you're on top of communication. "Let's ensure alignment across all teams."

Scalability
- Definition: A fancy way to talk about growth potential or whether an idea is worth the effort. Usage Tip: Mention it during brainstorming sessions to sound visionary. "We need to consider the scalability of this idea."

Optimize
- Definition: Making something better, or pretending you're improving things. Usage Tip: Use it to sound proactive, especially if nothing really needs fixing. "We need to optimize our processes."

Streamline
- Definition: Making a process simpler, or at least claiming to. Usage Tip: Sounds effective, even if no one knows how you're streamlining anything. Example: "Let's streamline our workflow to increase productivity."

Low-Hanging Fruit

- Definition: The easiest tasks that should be tackled first for quick wins. Usage Tip: Use this term to sound like you're prioritizing smartly. "Let's focus on the low-hanging fruit to show progress."

Moving the Needle

- Definition: Making an impact or progress (theoretically). Usage Tip: Great for exaggerating minor achievements. Example: "This initiative should really move the needle on engagement."

Value-Add

- Definition: Anything that theoretically makes the product, service, or company better. Usage Tip: Works well when justifying your work. "What's the value-add here?"

Core Competency

- Definition: The main skills or strengths of a team, department, or individual. Usage Tip: Use it to flatter people while subtly shifting work their way. "We should let Marketing handle that; it's their core competency."

Proactive

- Definition: Getting things done before they become a problem. Usage Tip: Overuse this one for brownie points. "Let's be proactive and get a head start on the report."

Take It Offline

- Definition: Discuss this issue privately or later (usually because it's unimportant or awkward). Usage Tip: A polite way to say, "This doesn't concern everyone." Example: "We'll take this offline after the meeting."

SECTION 1: MASTERING THE ART OF APPEARANCES

SECTION I: MASTERING THE ART OF APPEARANCES

THE THOUGHTFUL NOD

The "Thoughtful Nod" is one of the simplest yet most powerful tools in your arsenal for looking productive. Mastering this subtle gesture will make everyone around you feel like you're completely engaged, even if you're a bit lost.

The Thoughtful Nod focuses on timing, subtlety, and expression. It's more than just a head bob; it's a thoughtfully crafted performance that communicates, "I am fully engaged with what's going on here" while your thoughts drift off to dinner ideas or weekend plans.

HOW TO MASTER THE THOUGHTFUL NOD

Discover Your Groove
Take your time with the nod; consider it a soft acknowledgment instead of a spirited agreement. Try to maintain a steady, confident rhythm instead of looking like a bobblehead.

Add a gentle furrow to the brow.
To truly enhance the look, add a gentle furrow to your brow, as if you're thoughtfully processing the information. This will make it seem like you're really pondering something important.

Sometimes making eye contact
From time to time, make sure to lock eyes with the speaker to demonstrate that you're truly engaged with what they're saying. Making eye contact is great, but it's nice to keep it balanced so it doesn't feel too intense!

The Gentle Murmur
For advanced nodders, you can gently say phrases like "Absolutely" or "Good point" to make it even more effective. Maintain a gentle tone that feels intimate and thoughtful.

ACTIVITY: PRACTICE THE THOUGHTFUL NOD IN THE MIRROR

- Stand in front of a mirror and cheerfully recite random buzzwords like "synergy," "alignment," and "scalability" while nodding thoughtfully to each one. Encourage yourself to believe that you're truly soaking up amazing insights!
- Try out various angles of head tilt and brow furrowing until you discover a look that conveys, "I am truly engaged."

MINI CHALLENGE: THE NODDING COUNT

Next time you're in a meeting, why not have a little fun by seeing how many times you can nod thoughtfully while still keeping your mind wandering? It's a lighthearted challenge! Just a little reminder: nodding is great when others are sharing, but save your nods for when it's your turn to chime in!

STRATEGIC KEYBOARD TYPING

Sometimes, all it takes to appear focused is some enthusiastic, lively keyboard typing. The Strategic Keyboard Typing technique is perfect for looking totally focused on your work, no matter what's really on your screen. It's more about the vibe and the energy—the quicker and louder, the more fun!

GUIDE TO STRATEGIC KEYBOARD TYPING

Turn up the volume!
Let's type with intention! Show those keys who's in charge! The sound of quick typing can really set the mood for getting things done, so try to keep it steady and rhythmic to highlight your "work."

Combine the Patterns
Mix in some quick typing moments with longer pauses to give the impression of deep thinking and analysis. It's a fun idea to pause, gaze thoughtfully at the screen, and then jump back in with fresh energy!

Sometimes tilting the head and frowning
While you're typing away, take a moment to tilt your head a bit and squint at the screen, almost like you're figuring out a tricky puzzle. This shows that you're addressing an important matter.

The Rare "Hmm"

Every now and then, sprinkle in a gentle "Hmm..." or a soft "Interesting..." as if you've just stumbled upon something truly fascinating. It creates the impression of being deeply focused.

Practice Page: Typing Drill for "Intense Data Analysis"

For practice, go ahead and type the alphabet in a fun, out-of-order way to create your own "analysis session." Maintain a steady pace and turn up the volume!

Here's a fun way to practice your typing skills:

G R H K L D S A P Q M T W F V Z C X E B N Y J U
R V D T Y P Q N C X M L S K H G J E W Z A Q

Keep practicing this exercise until you can type random letters quickly and with great enthusiasm!

DESK DÉCOR FOR SUCCESS

Your desk can be a source of inspiration, even if your to-do list is a bit light. With the right decor, you can create a vibe of being "busy" all the time. Here's a checklist of items that say, "I'm really busy right now, but I'm working hard to solve all the company's problems!"

CHECKLIST: ESSENTIAL DESK ITEMS FOR A PRODUCTIVE VIBE

Planner You Don't Use

A beloved planner filled with cheerful scribbles and sticky notes peeking out. It's all about the appearance, so there's really no need to open it!

Sticky Notes featuring Fun Words

Place sticky notes around with fun phrases like "Deadline," "URGENT," or "Circle Back." If someone inquires, just say they're reminders for important projects you "can't talk about at the moment."

Partially Filled Coffee Mug

This is really important! A half-finished mug of coffee suggests you've been so busy that you haven't had a chance to enjoy your caffeine boost! It's a nice touch to have a mug with a motivational slogan like "Hustle Harder."

Unopened Stack of Papers

A stack of papers really boosts your "I'm so busy" vibe! Just be sure to keep anything personal off the top!

Calculator (Extra Points for Dust)

Even if you're in a non-math role, a calculator suggests you're diving into some serious number-crunching. Dust is optional for a little extra flair!

Printouts of Unopened Emails

Print a few important-looking emails and leave them out as if you plan to "get to them" later. Ensure the subjects are clear so everyone can appreciate how important your workload is.

Three Pens (One That's Run Out of Ink)

Place some pens around your desk to give the impression that you're always jotting down ideas. Ensure that one pen is out of ink to create a genuine, "I've been using this pen a lot" feel.

The One "Uplifting" Book

Have a leadership or self-help book on the corner of your desk, ideally with a few sticky notes peeking out. It gives the impression that you're constantly working towards bettering yourself.

With this setup and your Strategic Keyboard Typing, you'll appear to be the busiest person in the room, even if your main task of the day is just choosing lunch.

SECTION 2: NAVIGATING MEETINGS LIKE A PRO

SECTION 2: NAVIGATING MEETINGS LIKE A PRO

THE SERIOUS LISTENING FACE

Every experienced office professional understands that meetings often focus more on appearing engaged than truly soaking up the information. The Serious Listening Face is a handy addition to your "fake productivity" toolkit. Using the right expressions, you can show a deep sense of focus, even if your thoughts are wandering far away. Let's explore this by looking at three levels of engagement, ranging from a bit curious to really concerned.

PRACTICE EXERCISE: THE THREE LEVELS OF THE SERIOUS LISTENING FACE

Level 1: A Little Curious
Great for: Casual team meetings or routine updates. How to Make It Happen:

Soften your face, maintaining a gentle lift in your brow, as if you're engaged just enough to show you're paying attention without being impolite.
Give a little nod now and then to show you're engaged and following along.
Feel free to softly purse your lips and give your head a little tilt.

Level 2: Involved and Attentive

Great for: Those important meetings or discussions where folks might really hope you remember something. How to Make It Happen:

Gently furrow your brow to show that you're deep in thought.

Nod every 15-20 seconds, and add a gentle "Hmm" or "Yes, I see" to keep the conversation flowing.

Every now and then, jot down a quick note or even a doodle to show that you're thinking things through.

Level 3: Very Worried

Great for: Important meetings, budget talks, or any gathering with upper management. How to Make It Happen:

Try to deepen the brow furrow a bit, and perhaps add a gentle squint, as if you're carefully considering each word for its deeper significance.

Gently tilt your head and give your chin a little pinch now and then, like you're pondering something intriguing.

Incorporate gentle, thoughtful nods that convey, "I'm really considering this." Feel free to quietly say "Interesting..." or "That's a good point" from time to time.

MIRROR ACTIVITY: PERFECTING YOUR SERIOUS LISTENING FACE

1. Take a moment to stand in front of a mirror and give each level of the Serious Listening Face a try! Hold each expression for about 10 seconds, making small tweaks to your brow, mouth, and eye focus until you appear genuinely "engaged."

2. How would you **rate yourself** on each level?

Level 1: Does it seem like you're casually interested but at ease?
Level 2: Do you appear to be genuinely involved, as if you're really paying attention?
Level 3: Are you giving off a "deeply concerned" vibe, as if you're thinking about the future of the company?

3. Bonus Challenge: Try incorporating some fun gestures, like a head tilt or a quick "note-taking" moment, to elevate your Serious Listening Face from good to great.

With your Serious Listening Face perfected, you'll be all set to tackle any meeting with a vibe of quiet confidence, whether you're fully engaged or just looking forward to lunch.

PRETENDING TO TAKE NOTES

Writing down notes during a meeting shows that you're engaged and professional—like someone who's truly in the moment. But who really has the time for actual notes? Why not fill your notepad with some fun business buzzwords and catchy phrases?

You'll not only appear as the most dedicated employee in the room, but you'll also get to skip the hassle of remembering anything!

CHALLENGE: BUZZWORD-FILLED NOTE PAGE

Feel free to use these sample phrases to fill your page with "important" notes! You're welcome to mix and match for the best results! The aim is to give the impression of profound contemplation while not actually putting down anything significant.

Sample Phrases for Your Notes:
- "Circle back on that"
- "Next quarter priorities"
- "Let's leverage that"
- "Scalability of current strategies"
- "Address potential bottlenecks"
- "High-level alignment needed"
- "Optimize resources"
- "Discuss low-hanging fruit"
- "Key metrics and KPIs"
- "Possible synergy opportunities"
- "Actionable insights for Q3"
- "Strategic touchpoints"

Try writing down two or three of these phrases every few minutes, and mix up your handwriting to give the impression that you're "reacting" to new information. Add some checkmarks or arrows to enhance your message!

ADVANCED DOODLING TECHNIQUES

A truly skilled meeting attendee has a knack for adding a bit of doodling here and there without anyone noticing. Getting the hang of some simple doodles can really give the impression that you're sketching out intricate ideas or visualizing ways to enhance workflows. Here's a fun guide to making doodles that appear just productive enough!

DOODLE EXERCISE: DRAWING A "COMPLEX PROCESS MAP"

Spirals and Arrows

How about drawing a bunch of spirals in the margins and linking them up with some arrows? Sounds fun! This gives the feeling of a "process map" or a fun brainstorming session.

Change up the sizes of the spirals and play around with different arrow styles—dashed, dotted, bold—to represent various layers of thought.

Flowchart Boxes

How about drawing some empty boxes and connecting them with lines or arrows? That sounds fun! Label each box with terms that sound really impressive, such as "Action Plan," "Execution Phase," or "Follow-Up."

Add a few question marks or exclamation points near some arrows to highlight potential problem areas!

Circles and Connections

How about drawing some circles and connecting them with lines, just like a fun web? Label the circles with words such as "Resources," "Objectives," and "Stakeholders" to create a visual representation of interdepartmental relationships.
Scatter some random dots around the circles to create a fun "brainstorming" vibe!

PROMPT: CREATING YOUR PROCESS MAP DOODLE

Picture yourself creating a "complex process map" for a fun imaginary project. How about mixing spirals, arrows, and labeled boxes to create a fun and detailed workflow? Here are some example labels: "Phase 1," "Implementation," "Feedback Loop," and "End Goal." This doodle should resemble something right from a project management playbook!

Using these note-taking and doodling techniques, you'll appear ready to share an exciting business idea in every meeting. Who can say? You could totally inspire others to try out the buzzword-doodle method! Happy pretending!

SECTION 3: THE ART OF THE PERFECT REPLY-ALL

SECTION 3: THE ART OF THE PERFECT REPLY-ALL

REPLY-ALL ETIQUETTE

Getting the hang of the Reply-All is a key part of thriving in the office. There's nothing quite like getting a long email thread filled with "Thank you!" and "Noted" from everyone in the company. Understanding when to join in with your own Reply-All—and when to hold back—can really influence whether you're viewed as a supportive team member or an email bother.

Check out this guide to help you figure out if an email truly needs that dreaded Reply-All, along with a fun quiz to test your skills!

SCENARIO: RATE THE URGENCY OF THE REPLY-ALL

Scenario 1: Team Announcement
The manager sends a cheerful email to the team celebrating their achievement of reaching a project milestone.
Reply-All Urgency: Not a big deal
Tip: Try to avoid saying "Thank you, team!" Another "Yay!" in the inbox might not be what everyone is looking for.

Scenario 2: Need for Project Clarification

A team member reaches out to the entire team for more information about an assignment.

Reply-All Urgency: Moderate

Hey there! Just a quick tip: If you think others might have the same question, using Reply-All could really help save everyone some time. Feel free to respond directly!

Scenario 3: Celebrating Birthdays and Work Anniversaries

HR sends a cheerful email to celebrate someone's special day.

Reply to everyone Urgency: High (if you're in the holiday spirit)

Just a friendly reminder: a Reply-All with a quick "Happy Birthday!" or "Congrats!" can really brighten someone's day and is often appreciated! Just keep it balanced.

Scenario 4: Update on Company-Wide Policies

The HR team has shared an updated employee handbook and would love to hear your thoughts on it!

Reply-All There's no rush at all.

Hey there! Just a friendly reminder: if you don't see any big problems, it's best to avoid hitting Reply-All. People appreciate genuine feedback, so let's keep the inbox clear of just "Looks good!" messages.

Scenario 5: Quick Request for Resources

A coworker reaches out to the group, seeking some quick assistance on a project that has a deadline coming up soon.

Reply-All Urgency: Elevated

Tip: When time is tight, using Reply-All can be a great way to show that you're ready to lend a hand!

QUIZ: "IS THIS REALLY A REPLY-ALL?"

Answer "Yes" or "No" to determine whether a Reply-All is really necessary for each email scenario.

An email from IT reminding everyone to reset their passwords.

- Answer: No
- Explanation: No one needs your "Got it!" cluttering their inbox.

A group email from your boss asking for updates on project progress by end of day.

- Answer: Yes
- Explanation: A quick Reply-All to confirm your update or completion shows accountability (but only if everyone's input is relevant).

A colleague asks everyone for input on what kind of snacks should be ordered for the next team meeting.

- Answer: Yes
- Explanation: Go ahead and let your snack preference be known—team morale depends on it!

The CEO sends a congratulatory message to the team for the quarter's success.

- Answer: No

- Explanation: Resist the urge. Everyone appreciates the sentiment, but a single "Thank you" email is usually enough.

An email thread discussing the office holiday party theme, with a request for costume ideas.
- Answer: Yes
- Explanation: Everyone loves a fun email thread! Just make sure your suggestion is thoughtful or funny.

Final Tip: If you're ever unsure about hitting Reply-All, picture everyone getting your email and think, "Will this brighten their day a bit, or just add to the clutter?" If it's a bit messy, just respond directly instead. With a bit of practice, you'll get the hang of sending the perfectly timed Reply-All!

CREATING MEANINGFUL EMAIL SIGN-OFFS

A nicely crafted email sign-off is like the cherry on top of your message—a final, memorable touch that really makes an impression. While traditional sign-offs like "Best regards" or "Sincerely" are perfectly fine, why not choose something a bit more special? Here's your opportunity to shine with a professional-sounding (and a bit playful) email closer that will either impress or amuse your colleagues.

ACTIVITY: INVENTING YOUR SIGNATURE SIGN-OFF

Feel free to draw from these ideas to create a distinctive closing line that combines professionalism with a touch of personality. Give them a go and find the one that suits you best!

1. Synergy Specialist
- Sign-Off: "Best Synergistically,"
- Perfect for: Emails full of buzzwords that make you sound like a corporate powerhouse.

2. The Hard Worker's Farewell
- Sign-Off: "Warm regards, the hardest worker"
- Perfect for: Subtly reminding everyone of your "dedication" to the company.

3. The Reliable Follow-Upper
- Sign-Off: "Yours in Alignment,"
- Perfect for: Emails where you want to emphasize that you're always in sync with team goals.

4. The Innovator's Goodbye
- Sign-Off: "In pursuit of optimization,"
- Perfect for: Emails where you've offered a fresh idea or improvement suggestion.

5. The Deadline Devotee
- Sign-Off: "Yours in Timely Execution,"
- Perfect for: Project updates or deadline reminders where you want to showcase your commitment.

6. The Buzzword Enthusiast
- Sign-Off: "Best Leverage,"
- Perfect for: Sending emails packed with corporate jargon to subtly reinforce your "strategic thinking."

7. The Work-Life Balance Guru
- Sign-Off: "Mindfully yours,"
- Perfect for: Emailing after-hours or reminding colleagues that balance matters—even if you're glued to your screen.

8. The Go-Getter's Adieu
- Sign-Off: "Full steam ahead,"
- Perfect for: Closing emails that emphasize your proactive approach.

9. The Empathetic Colleague
- Sign-Off: "With team spirit,"
- Perfect for: Emails addressing group projects or shared goals to show you're all in.

10. The Data-Driven Professional
- Sign-Off: "In pursuit of actionable insights,"
- Perfect for: Sending out analytical reports or anything with numbers (even if you made half of them up).

TEMPLATE PRACTICE: CHOOSING YOUR IDEAL EMAIL SIGN-OFF

Complete the blanks to create your ideal sign-off:

"[Your chosen adjective or phrase], [Your catchy closing phrase]."

For instance:

- "Strategically yours, keeping synergy alive,"
- "With optimized intentions, your data champion,"
- "In alignment, your results-oriented colleague,"

Have fun trying out different combinations until you discover the one that feels perfect for you! Once you've chosen your signature sign-off, get ready to hit send with confidence and a touch of flair!

SECTION 4: COFFEE BREAK CAMOUFLAGE

SECTION 4: COFFEE BREAK CAMOUFLAGE

MASTERING THE "JUST GRABBING A COFFEE" EXCUSE

Coffee breaks are more than just a caffeine fix—they're a perfect chance to take a little breather, enjoy a mid-morning refresh, or even a clever way to sidestep some extra tasks. It's all about making your coffee outings feel like a great use of your time! Here's a fun way to perfect the "Just Grabbing a Coffee" excuse with some convincing reasons that will make your trip to the coffee machine feel absolutely necessary.

EXERCISE: WRITING OUT "IMPORTANT" REASONS FOR A COFFEE RUN

Feel free to use these examples, or get creative and come up with your own, to make each coffee break feel essential for boosting your productivity.

- "I need a quick recharge before diving into [important task]"
- Effectiveness:
- Why It Works: Suggests you're about to take on a major task and need a little boost to get into the zone.

- "I'm grabbing a coffee before our big [meeting name]"
- Effectiveness:
- Why It Works: Aligns your coffee run with preparation for an upcoming event, making it sound like part of your productivity ritual.
- "Just clearing my head to tackle that report"
- Effectiveness:
- Why It Works: A coffee break sounds like an essential reset to prepare for focused work. This is good for small breaks, but best not to overuse.
- "Need to refuel—lots of analysis ahead!"
- Effectiveness:
- Why It Works: Makes it sound like you're about to tackle a challenging, brain-intensive task and can't do it without a cup in hand.
- "Getting coffee to brainstorm some ideas"
- Effectiveness:
- Why It Works: Suggests you're not only working but being creatively strategic—good for sending the signal that you're constantly thinking ahead.
- "Heading for a coffee so I can be sharp for the client call"
- Effectiveness:
- Why It Works: Perfect for when you're about to interface with clients, making it clear you want to be on top of your game. Everyone understands the need for a little extra focus!

- "Getting a quick coffee to prep for end-of-day tasks"
- Effectiveness:
- Why It Works: Shows you're pacing yourself to be productive all day, even if the end of the day is actually more about winding down.
- "Need a quick break to avoid burnout—lots to finish up today!"
- Effectiveness:
- Why It Works: Shows awareness of self-care and time management, which is relatable and responsible.

Here are some friendly guidelines:

-         - Perfect: It really captures the essence of being dedicated to work and shows a strong commitment to the job.
-         - Great: A solid excuse, but it could use a bit of variety if it's used frequently.
-         - Good: Works well when used in moderation, but it might feel a bit repetitive if you use it too much.
-         - Risky: It's on the edge, and a more specific or urgent angle could help it feel more credible.

Why not whip up some of your own and blend them together for a fun twist! Before you know it, you'll be the expert at taking perfectly timed coffee breaks, and everyone will believe that each visit is a clever part of your success plan.

THE ART OF RETURNING WITH A PURPOSE

A great coffee break is not only about taking a little time away, but also about coming back refreshed. Returning to your desk with a sense of purpose and focus makes it seem like your coffee break was a valuable moment for inspiration and problem-solving. Check out these tips to give the impression that you've had a life-changing realization while visiting the coffee machine.

GUIDE: TIPS ON RETURNING FROM A COFFEE BREAK WITH CONVICTION

The Focused Walk

Instead of casually walking back to your desk, try to move with purpose and a thoughtful expression, as if you're deep in contemplation. This look expresses, "I've just had a revelation, and I'm excited to take action!"

The "Aha!" Face

As you settle in, feel free to let out a soft "Ah!" or "Of course!" as if a light bulb just went off. Taking a moment to nod thoughtfully as you get comfortable can really enhance the experience.

The Quick Scribble

Keep a notebook or a sticky note close by. Once you take a seat, go ahead and start writing something, whether it's a real note or just some fun keywords. Try to capture that spark of brilliance before it slips away!

The Relaxed Announcement

Once you're all settled in, you might want to casually share with a coworker nearby, "I just had an idea about [insert project] while I was getting my coffee." This can lead to great conversations and make your coffee breaks feel productive, even a bit inspiring!

The Committed Typing

Get ready to type or click with enthusiasm, as if you're bringing your exciting new "breakthrough" idea to life! This busy return to work makes it seem like your coffee break was a game changer for getting things done.

ACTIVITY: BRAINSTORM THREE "GAME-CHANGING" IDEAS TO MENTION POST-COFFEE BREAK

Pick a couple of these "revolutionary" ideas to casually mention in conversation or discuss in a meeting. They don't need to be revolutionary—just enough to feel proactive and considerate.

"I was thinking, maybe we could create a weekly 'productivity pulse' check-in for the team."

- Why It Works: Suggests you're focused on keeping the team aligned and motivated. Bonus points if you add, "I think it could really streamline communication."

"What if we add a 'quick wins' section to our project updates?"

- Why It Works: This idea sounds actionable, but vague enough that you can refine it later. Mentioning "quick wins" gives off a solution-oriented vibe.

"I've been considering how we could optimize [specific process]. I think a small tweak could improve efficiency."

- Why It Works: It sounds like you're already thinking critically about workflows and looking for ways to improve.

"It occurred to me that we could introduce a 'mini brainstorming' session at the end of each team meeting."

- Why It Works: This suggests that you value team input and want to encourage more collaborative problem-solving.

"I thought of a way we could leverage [specific tool/software] more effectively for our team goals."

- Why It Works: Makes it look like you're always seeking ways to improve productivity by optimizing existing resources.

"We could introduce a 'monthly reflection' to see how our strategies are aligning with our goals."

- Why It Works: Sounds like a high-level suggestion aimed at keeping the team on track without adding much extra work for yourself.

"What if we revisit our client feedback system? There might be a way to streamline it and make responses more actionable."

- Why It Works: Shows that you're focused on continuous improvement and client satisfaction.

Choose three ideas that feel just right for your workplace, or feel free to create your own variations! The aim is to ensure that when you come back from your coffee break, it feels like you've just ignited your next great idea. Before long, your coffee breaks will be known as the perfect time for sparking your "innovative" ideas!

SECTION 5: HANDLING THE BOSS DRIVE-BY

THE INSTANT SWITCH TO "PRODUCTIVE MODE"

One of the most important skills for thriving in any office is the knack for jumping into "Productive Mode" as soon as your boss comes around. Whether you're browsing online, catching up on the latest gossip, or planning your next vacation, getting the hang of quick tab-switching can really give the impression that you've been deeply focused on work all along.

Check out this guide to mastering the "Instant Switch" technique, along with a fun challenge to put your reflexes to the test!

PRACTICE DRILL: TIPS ON THE QUICK SWITCH TO PRODUCTIVITY

Keep a "Safe" Tab Open!

It's a great idea to keep a "work-related" tab open—like an Excel sheet, a project document, or an email draft—so you're always ready to jump in! This is your quick switch destination!

Place Your Tabs Thoughtfully

Put your "safe" work tab right next to the fun things, like social media or shopping! With just one click, you can easily switch back to work mode!

Try using keyboard shortcuts!

You can easily switch between open applications using Alt + Tab on Windows or Command + Tab on Mac. Give these shortcuts a try until they feel like second nature!

Get the hang of the Quick Scroll!

If you're working on something a bit less interactive, like a report, scrolling back and forth can give the impression that you're double-checking details. Include a considerate head tilt to enhance your credibility.

Position Your Screen Thoughtfully

Adjust your screen so it's easy to see but still has a bit of privacy. This way, you'll have just a little extra time to react when you see your boss coming your way.

The "Typing for Emphasis" Trick

Once you switch to your safe tab, go ahead and start typing like you're entering some important data or notes! Feel free to type anything you like—just keep it lively!

REACTION TIME CHALLENGE: THE QUICK SWITCH TEST

It's time to put your reflexes to the test! Check out how quickly you can move from a fun tab, like social media, to a spreadsheet! Here's a friendly little guide for the challenge:

Get Your Screen Ready

Open a fun tab for some light browsing, like social media, news, or online shopping!
Just beside it, go ahead and open an Excel sheet or another work-related tab.

Get Ready for Success

Take a moment to unwind and enjoy your time in that "distraction" tab. Why not set a timer or have a buddy cheer you on with a "Go!"?

The Switch

When you hear "Go," swiftly move from your distraction tab to the Excel sheet. Go ahead and start scrolling or typing to give the impression that you're engaged in data analysis!

Track Your Time

Try using a timer to find out how fast you can switch from "fun mode" to "work mode." Try to keep it under two seconds! With a bit of practice, you could even get it down to under one second!

TIPS FOR IMPROVEMENT

Muscle Memory:

Keep practicing your keyboard shortcuts until they feel completely natural. The quicker you can tap those keys, the better it will be!

Quick Reactions:

Picture this – you hear your boss's footsteps coming your way and see how fast you can respond!

Polish Your "Work Face":

Ensure your expression is focused while you type or scroll. Giving a little furrowed brow or a head tilt can really make a difference!

With these skills, you'll effortlessly switch to "Productive Mode" in no time, keeping your reputation as an ultra-focused employee—even when you're just one tab away from some fun!

"LET ME GET BACK TO YOU ON THAT" - THE PERFECT DELAYING PHRASE

When your boss surprises you with a question or request, responding quickly isn't always the best way to go. Sometimes, giving yourself a bit of extra time can be really helpful. "Let me get back to you on that" is a friendly and flexible phrase that shows you're engaged without making a promise for an immediate response. This phrase and its variations can be really helpful when you need them!

EXERCISE: MATCHING DELAY PHRASES TO COMMON OFFICE SCENARIOS

Select the most suitable delay phrase for every situation. Get the hang of these responses, and you'll have a great way to buy some time in just about any situation!

1. **Situation:** The boss is checking in on the progress of a project that you've just begun.

Great Delay Phrase: "I'll need to double-check my notes to ensure I have the most up-to-date details."
Reasons for Its Effectiveness: It suggests that you're careful and attentive to the little things.

2. **Scenario:** Your manager is looking for a clear answer on a budget question, but you're uncertain about the figures.

Best Delay Phrase: "I'll need to check those numbers to confirm." I'll be in touch with you shortly!

Here's Why It Works: Signs that you handle numbers responsibly and should double-check the data.

3. **Scenario:** Hey! Thanks for thinking of me, but I have to pass on the meeting this time. Hope it goes well!

Great delay phrase: "Let me check my calendar, and I'll circle back."

Reasons for Its Effectiveness: It allows you to think about whether it's something you'd like to be a part of or to find a reason to pass on it.

4. **Situation:** The team requests that you take charge of a task that doesn't really excite you.

Great Delay Phrase: "I'll need to check if I have the capacity for that this week."

Here's Why It Works: It conveys a professional vibe and shows that you're occupied, even if that's not the case.

5. **Scenario:** You're asked for a quick decision on a minor detail, but you'd prefer to hold off on making a commitment.

Great Delay Phrase: "Let me give that some thought and get back to you."

It demonstrates that you take your time to think things through and consider even the little things before making decisions.

ACTIVITY: CREATE YOUR OWN DELAY PHRASES

Come up with your own takes on the classic phrase "Let me get back to you on that" for various situations. Feel free to take your time to gather your thoughts and come up with at least three phrases that sound both natural and professional.

EXAMPLES OF CUSTOM DELAY PHRASES:

"I'd like to gather more information on that before giving a response."
- Great for: Vague questions that need more context (or give you an excuse to ask for details you didn't catch).

"I'll need to review our guidelines to make sure we're in alignment."
- Great for: Situations that require you to check policies or verify information, even if you just need to stall.

"I want to make sure I'm covering all the bases—let me look into it and follow up."
- Great for: Any time you want to show that you're thorough, even if the issue isn't urgent.

TEMPLATE FOR CRAFTING YOUR OWN DELAY PHRASE

Here's a fun fill-in-the-blank template to help you come up with new delay phrases for different situations:

"I'll need to [action phrase, e.g., check my notes, review the data, look into it] to [reason for delay, e.g., ensure accuracy, confirm alignment, get the latest details]. I'll get back to you soon."

Try out various combinations to discover the perfect tone for your workplace! Before long, you'll have a handy set of delay phrases that will make you seem thoughtful and meticulous, even if you're just taking a moment to gather your thoughts.

SECTION 6: THE SCIENCE OF SOUNDING SMART

SECTION 6: THE SCIENCE OF SOUNDING SMART

MEMORIZING BUSINESS JARGON

In the realm of office communication, using the right buzzwords can really help you come across as the smartest person in the room—even if you're not entirely clear on their meanings. Getting the hang of a few helpful phrases can really make a difference in how you handle meetings, emails, and presentations. Terms like "paradigm shift" and "actionable insights" can really boost how others see your expertise, so let's explore some of the best jargon to weave into our conversations.

ACTIVITY: BUZZWORD WORD SEARCH

See if you can spot the office buzzwords tucked away in the puzzle below! These words are among the most commonly used (and often misunderstood) terms in corporate culture. Once you can easily spot these terms, you'll be all set to incorporate them into your everyday vocabulary!

```
A M J P T P Z W D L E V E R A G E B L J
C E A L I G N M E N T K N I Z H S P U V
T P Q O O T C X V I M L S W T I T A Y Z
I U R I P T A V V I P O Y N I G R R O C
O D Z L U T J U Z A K U G T P E A A I S
N K S M U E I P W C L Y F M F K T D Z C
A P G T E J K M A P S U A G D Q E I C A
B Q L R R U T B I U G O E O U L G G O L
L M I A W E E F G Z R M G A T Y I M R A
E F P B N L A C B I A Z J D D D C S E B
I A F X C X V M Z F S T Q Y K D G H C I
N Q T R O H L G L Y C X I C P F O I O L
S S I R B A N D W I D T H O I K A F M I
I C Q P B J F P B R N W N U N E L T P T
G N C Z G T N V Y I J E A W S O S I E Y
H R M P F O K C T O U C H P O I N T T L
T I Z W R I T K S Q M S Y N E R G Y E B
S Z L T E V P I X Q U M U U P D E G N K
H E Q O S P A Z G E O L C R I T U J C W
R O M L O W H A N G I N G F R U I T Y E
```

ACTIONABLE INSIGHTS	ALIGNMENT
BANDWIDTH	CIRCLE BACK
CORE COMPETENCY	LEVERAGE
LOW-HANGING FRUIT	OPTIMIZATION
PARADIGM SHIFT	SCALABILITY
STRATEGIC GOALS	STREAMLINE
SYNERGY	TOUCHPOINT
VALUE-ADD	

Once you finish the word search, you'll have learned some key buzzwords that you can start using in conversation, instantly enhancing your credibility!

```
A M J P T P Z W D (L E V E R A G E) B L J
C E (A L I G N M E N T) K N I Z H S P U V
T P Q (O) O T C X V I M L S W T I T A Y Z
I U R I (P) T A V (V) I P O Y N I G R R O C
O D Z L U (T) J U Z (A K) U G T P E A A I S
N K S M U E (I) P W (C L) Y F M F K T D Z C
A P G (T) E J K (M A) P S U A G D Q E I C A
B Q L (R) R U T (B I) U G O E O U L G G O L
L M I A W (E E) F G (Z) R M G (A) T Y I M R A
E F P B N (L A) C B I (A) Z J D D D C S E B
I A F X (C X) V M Z F S (T) Q Y K D G H C I
N Q T (R O) H L G (L) Y C X (I) C P F O I O L
S (I) R (B A N D W I D T H O) I K A F M I I
I (C) Q P B J F P B R (N) W N U N E L T P T
G N C Z G T N V Y I J (E) A W S O S I E Y
H R M P F O K C (T O U C H P O I N T) T L
T I Z W R I T K S Q M (S Y N E R G Y) E B
S Z L T E V P I X Q U M U U P D E G N K
H E Q O S P A Z G E O L C R I T U J C W
R O M (L O W H A N G I N G F R U I T) Y E
```

PUZZLE SOLUTION

ASKING QUESTIONS THAT MAKE YOU SOUND SMART

Asking questions in a meeting is a great way to show that you're engaged and thoughtful, even if your question doesn't necessarily add new information. A well-crafted question can really showcase your thoughtful and strategic thinking, allowing you to consider all angles without having to get into the nitty-gritty details.

Here are a few examples of questions that might sound profound but don't really convey much in the end. Make sure to use them thoughtfully to convey a sense of intelligence and curiosity!

EXAMPLES OF SMART-SOUNDING QUESTIONS

"Have we considered all touchpoints?"
- Why It Works: This question implies that you're thinking about every possible angle and connection, even if no one's quite sure what "all touchpoints" entails.

"What's our long-term strategy for scalability on this?"
- Why It Works: A good go-to question when discussing growth or expansion, even if you don't need specific details. It makes you sound like you're looking at the big picture.

"Have we considered all touchpoints?"

- Why It Works: This question implies that you're thinking about every possible angle and connection, even if no one's quite sure what "all touchpoints" entails.

"What's our long-term strategy for scalability on this?"

- Why It Works: A good go-to question when discussing growth or expansion, even if you don't need specific details. It makes you sound like you're looking at the big picture.

"How does this align with our overall mission and values?"

- Why It Works: This question shows that you're focused on the organization's core principles, adding weight to the discussion without getting into specifics.

"Are we optimizing for efficiency or for impact here?"

- Why It Works: By framing the question as a choice between two high-level goals, you appear strategic and thoughtful about priorities.

"What are the key metrics we're using to measure success?"

- Why It Works: This question suggests you're detail-oriented and results-focused, even if you don't plan on following up on those metrics.

PRACTICE EXERCISE: WRITING YOUR OWN "DEEP" QUESTIONS

It's your turn now! Come up with three thought-provoking questions to share at your next meeting.

Keep them a bit vague yet strategic, so they can work in almost any situation.

Prompts to Get Started:
- "How are we ensuring alignment with [project/goal] across all departments?"
- "Is there a plan to address potential bottlenecks as we move forward?"
- "What opportunities do we have for leveraging existing resources here?"

Example Questions:

1. **"What risks or dependencies should we be mindful of as we proceed?"**
   - Perfect for sounding cautious and forward-thinking without needing to identify specific risks.

2. **"Have we explored all potential avenues for cross-functional collaboration on this?"**
   - Great for hinting that you're focused on teamwork, even if you don't have anyone specific in mind.

3. **"How will we measure the intangible benefits of this project?"**
   - Sounds impressive and results-oriented, with a hint of philosophical depth—ideal for any project with "soft" benefits.

With these clever questions in your toolkit, you'll be all set to leave a lasting impression in any meeting. Simply sprinkle one or two of these into the conversation, and you'll see everyone nodding in agreement, appreciating your insightful viewpoint.

SECTION 7: DISGUISING DOWNTIME

SECTION 7: DISGUISING DOWNTIME

EFFICIENT "RESEARCH BROWSING"

Sometimes, it's nice to take a little break from work without feeling like you're not getting things done. Let's dive into some research browsing! This art is all about exploring websites that seem really work-related, helping you look focused and knowledgeable, even if you're just enjoying some downtime. Keeping a list of "safe" sites handy will make it easy to enjoy your downtime while still looking professional.

CHECKLIST: WEBSITES THAT LOOK LIKE WORK

Here's a great list of websites that are just right for some enjoyable "research browsing." Every one of them has a professional look that could fit well in nearly any job setting. Make sure to bookmark these for easy access!

1. **News Sites in the Industry**

Here are some examples: Financial Times, Forbes, TechCrunch, Bloomberg
Reasons for Its Effectiveness: Keeping "up-to-date" with industry news is something that can benefit nearly everyone in their job.

2. Learning and Growth Platforms

Some great options include LinkedIn Learning, Coursera, and Harvard Business Review.

Here's Why It Works: Exploring leadership skills, productivity tips, or the latest industry trends always feels like a great use of time.

3. Data and Analytics Tools

Here are some examples: Google Analytics, Data Studio, and Excel tutorial sites.

Reasons for Its Effectiveness: It seems like you're getting better at your data skills or diving into performance metrics!

4. Excel Templates and Tools

Here are some great options: Spreadsheet templates for managing projects, tools for finance, and planners for budgeting.

Reasons for Its Effectiveness: Checking out Excel templates or exploring new spreadsheet functions can often be seen as "workflow optimization."

5. Company Blogs and Whitepapers

Examples include top companies in your field or those you collaborate with.

Reasons It's Effective: Company blogs often share insights into industry trends, giving the impression that you're engaging in market research or competitive analysis.

6. Networking Platforms

Example: LinkedIn (for enjoying articles or discovering thought leadership content)
Reasons for Its Effectiveness: Connecting with others and exploring industry insights on LinkedIn can show that you're engaged in learning and staying updated with trends in your field.

7. Websites for Productivity and Project Management

Here are some examples: Asana, Trello, Notion. Let's explore why these tools are effective: Exploring project management tools shows that you're working on enhancing your organizational skills!

8. Exploring the Market and Industry

Here are some examples: Statista, Pew Research, or sites that focus on specific industries.

Here's why it works: Checking out market data is super helpful and helps you stay "informed" about the latest trends.

ACTIVITY: FILLING A "RESEARCH LOG" WITH OFFICIAL-SOUNDING TITLES

The next time you're diving into "research mode," consider keeping a research log with titles that sound impressive and professional! Writing these down really helps you feel connected to the important work you're doing.

SAMPLE RESEARCH LOG TITLES:

1. "Analyzing Trends in Remote Work and Employee Productivity"
2. "Exploring Key Performance Indicators in Cross-Functional Projects"
3. "Innovations in Data-Driven Decision Making for [Your Industry]"
4. "Emerging Tools for Workflow Optimization and Team Management"
5. "Current Market Trends and Their Impact on Our Business Strategy"
6. "Best Practices for Enhancing Client Satisfaction in [Your Field]"
7. "Review of Competitor Strategies in the Digital Landscape"
8. "Exploring Synergy Opportunities with New CRM Technologies"
9. "Data-Driven Insights for Effective Time Management"
10. "Evaluating Strategic Growth Metrics and Success Indicators"

Make sure to add a few of these titles to your log each week, and keep it visible as a gentle showcase of your "research." Soon, everyone will see you as a dedicated professional who's always exploring industry insights—even if you're actually just enjoying a well-deserved break.

THE FAKE DEADLINE HUSTLE

One of the best ways to seem busy—and steer clear of extra tasks—is to create a sense of urgency around a made-up deadline. The Fake Deadline Hustle is all about creating a task that seems really important and urgent, so you can appear busy and engaged. If done well, this approach can help prevent others from adding more tasks and might even earn you some extra respect for your hard work and dedication.

CHALLENGE: CREATE A DEADLINE THAT SOUNDS IMPORTANT

Your imaginary deadline should:

- Clear deadlines are much more convincing. Include some specifics about the "project" to enhance its persuasiveness.
- Looks important, but not pressing right now: Pick a deadline that encourages focus without being so close that someone feels the need to ask for an update right away.

- Pick a task that only you or a small team are involved in, ensuring that there's no possibility for anyone else to verify it.

EXAMPLES OF BELIEVABLE FAKE DEADLINES:

1. **"I've got to wrap up the preliminary analysis for the quarterly project review by Thursday."**
- Why It Works: "Preliminary analysis" and "quarterly project review" sound serious and could apply to almost any role.
2. **"I'm preparing the draft for the client feedback summary due next week."**
- Why It Works: "Client feedback summary" is specific, sounds like an important responsibility, and implies that you'll be busy until it's done.
3. **"I'm under a tight timeline to finalize the strategic report on [insert project name] by Friday."**
- Why It Works: Adding "strategic report" and a project name suggests high importance and urgency.
4. **"I have to submit the metrics report for internal review by Monday morning."**
- Why It Works: "Metrics report" sounds specific, and "internal review" adds a layer of accountability.

TEMPLATE: CRAFT YOUR OWN "URGENT TASK"

Feel free to use this template to set a believable deadline for your creative project:

"I need to [task action, e.g., finalize, prepare, wrap up] the [specific task or report name, e.g., preliminary analysis, client summary, metrics report] by [specific day or timeframe]."

Here are a few more examples based on this template:
1. "I need to finalize the content review report by end-of-day Thursday."
2. "I'm preparing the initial proposal draft for the cross-functional team by tomorrow."
3. "I've got to wrap up the budget breakdown summary for leadership by Friday."

Once you've crafted your fake deadline, mention it casually in conversation with colleagues or your boss. You could say, "I'd love to help, but I'm under a tight timeline to finish [your fake task] by [deadline day]." With your fake deadline in place, you'll have a buffer of uninterrupted time to take it easy or focus on something else—guilt-free!

SECTION 8: EXPERT-LEVEL PROCRASTINATION

PERFECTING THE "IN-BETWEEN TASK" LOOK

The "In-Between Task" Look is a clever way to seem really focused, even when you're in between tasks—or maybe just taking a little break from them. This look seems to show that you're taking a moment to collect your thoughts before jumping into the next exciting project. It strikes just the right balance between being active and taking a moment to reflect, and it clearly communicates: I'm busy, but I'm really focused.

CHALLENGE: MASTER THE IN-BETWEEN TASK LOOK

Here's how to embrace the "In-Between Task" look with confidence and grace:

Hold a Pen Thoughtfully
- Grip a pen lightly in one hand, as if you're about to jot down an important insight. Occasionally tap it gently on the notepad to give the impression that you're thinking things through.

Open a Notepad with Random Scribbles
- Keep a notepad in front of you with a few scribbles, bullet points, or half-written sentences. It should look like you've been taking notes and are preparing to dive back in.

Wear a Thoughtful Expression

- Tilt your head slightly and furrow your brow, as if weighing the details of an imaginary task. Avoid looking around the room—keep your gaze focused, ideally on the notepad or some undefined spot just past it.

Add the Occasional "Hmmm" or Nod

- Every so often, nod slightly or let out a quiet "Hmmm..." to suggest that you're connecting the dots in your mind.

Keep it Brief

- The beauty of the "In-Between Task" look is in its subtlety. Hold the pose for a few minutes before "switching" back to work mode. This keeps it looking natural, as if you're just resetting between big tasks.

ACTIVITY: SKETCH YOURSELF IN PEAK "IN-BETWEEN TASK" MODE

For fun, try sketching a quick image of yourself in this peak "In-Between Task" pose. If you're not an artist, no worries—this mental image alone will help you embody the ultimate "In-Between Task" vibe. With a bit of practice, you'll look like you're always on the verge of a major breakthrough, even during moments of well-deserved downtime.

YOUR SKETCH:

CREATING "DO NOT DISTURB" SIGNALS

When you need uninterrupted time—or just a little quiet downtime—a "Do Not Disturb" signal can be a lifesaver. Rather than telling your coworkers outright that you need a break, craft subtle, professional phrases that suggest you're deeply engaged in a critical task. This way, you create a buffer of quiet time without raising any suspicions.

EXERCISE: CRAFTING YOUR "DO NOT DISTURB" PHRASES

Here are a few versatile phrases that give the impression of intense focus or high-stakes work. Try these out or create your own for a gentle way to keep interruptions at bay.

"I'm in deep focus mode—can we connect later?"
- Perfect for: Setting boundaries while sounding impressively focused.

"I'm working on something time-sensitive right now; I'll circle back soon."
- Perfect for: Suggesting that you're on a tight deadline and can't be disturbed.

"Currently dissecting some complex data—let's touch base later."
- Perfect for: Adding a layer of mystery and importance, implying your task is not easily interrupted.

'I'm just wrapping up a thought—give me a few minutes!"

- Perfect for: Letting someone know you're at a crucial point in your "work," even if it's just your favorite playlist.

"Focused on deliverables—let's connect this afternoon."

- Perfect for: Vaguely pointing to important tasks, ideal for postponing less-urgent interruptions.

"In the middle of a creative brainstorming session—catch up soon!"

- Perfect for: Implying you're on the brink of a "breakthrough" idea and can't afford distractions.

MY "DO NOT DISTURB" PHRASES:

ACTIVITY: DESIGN YOUR IDEAL "DO NOT DISTURB" DOOR SIGN

For a fun twist, create your ideal "Do Not Disturb" sign. Visualize or draw it with creativity and humor—this is your perfect companion for keeping distractions to a minimum.

Suggested Elements for Your Door Sign:

- Bold, Clear Header: Something like "Deep Work Mode" or "On a Critical Task."
- Subtle Warning Line: "Please Disturb Only If Urgent" or "Silent Productivity Zone."
- Optional Humor: Add a line like "Thinking Big Thoughts," "Analyzing Critical Data," or "Innovation in Progress."
- Icons or Graphics: Small icons like a brain, magnifying glass, or even a light bulb to give it a professional but playful vibe.

Examples:

Deep Focus Mode**Innovation in ProgressPlease Disturb Only If Urgent

Quiet Zone** Currently Brainstorming Big Ideas Check Back in 10 Minutes

MY DO NOT DISTURB SIGN:

FINAL SECTION: THE ULTIMATE BOSS-IMPRESSION KIT

FINAL SECTION: THE ULTIMATE BOSS-IMPRESSION KIT

END-OF-DAY DESK TIDY-UP CHECKLIST

Leaving your desk at the end of the day should give the impression that you've been in full productivity mode from start to finish. A carefully "staged" desk can suggest dedication, focus, and a day well spent—even if most of it was spent strategically appearing busy. Here's your guide to leaving just the right amount of "clues" that you've had a jam-packed workday.

GUIDE: THE ART OF THE END-OF-DAY DESK LOOK

Create the "Busy but Organized" Look
- Your desk should appear like a whirlwind of productive activity just settled down. Scatter a few items strategically, but not chaotically. Think "mid-project" rather than "total mess."

Leave a Few Key Documents in View
- Keep some open folders or printed documents visible with notes or sticky tabs sticking out, as if they're ready to be tackled first thing tomorrow.

A Coffee Mug with Coffee Stains
- A half-empty coffee mug or a cup with a visible ring stain shows you were so engrossed in work that you barely noticed your drink cooling down.

Strategically Placed Sticky Notes

- Place sticky notes around your monitor or on documents with phrases like "Follow Up," "Urgent," or "Priority." They signal that you're managing multiple tasks.

An Open Spreadsheet or Email Draft

- Leave your computer screen on an open spreadsheet, complex chart, or a half-written email. This gives the impression that you were pulled away right in the middle of something important.

Pens, Notebooks, and Scribbles

- Scatter a couple of pens and a notepad with some quick notes or doodles. Bonus points if there's a page with random buzzwords like "strategy," "growth," and "leverage" scrawled across.

A Planner Open to Today's Date

- Open your planner to today's date, with a few items checked off and others not. This shows that while you made progress, there's still a lot on your plate.

Leave a Browser Tab Open to a Work-Related Site

- If you leave your computer unlocked, have a credible site open—like an industry news page, a data dashboard, or a report. It's all about looking immersed in work until the very last moment.

END OF THE DAY
Checklist

- ✓ Coffee mug (half-empty or with a visible coffee ring)
- ✓ Sticky notes with key words like "Follow-Up" or "Urgent"
- ✓ Open folder or stack of papers with a few "in-progress" notes
- ✓ Pens and notebook with doodles or quick notes
- ✓ Computer screen open to an important-looking document, spreadsheet, or email draft
- ✓ Planner open to today's page, with partially checked-off items
- ✓ Browser tab left open to something work-related, like an industry site or spreadsheet

FINAL SECTION: FINAL EXAM: ARE YOU READY TO FAKE PRODUCTIVITY LIKE A PRO?

Congratulations on making it to the final exam! Now it's time to test everything you've learned about looking busy, sounding smart, and mastering the subtle art of office survival. This quiz will put your newfound skills to the test with real-life scenarios, helping you prove that you're ready to fake productivity like a pro.

QUIZ: OFFICE SURVIVAL SITUATIONS

For each situation, choose the best response based on your expert-level office camouflage skills. Keep track of your answers to see if you've truly mastered the art of faking productivity.

Your boss stops by and asks what you're working on while you're taking a quick social media break. You should...
A) Quickly say "Oh, just taking a short mental break" and close the browser.
B) Switch to a work-related spreadsheet and start typing numbers randomly.
C) Say, "I'm researching best practices for our next project" and proceed to LinkedIn for "networking."

You're not prepared for an impromptu project meeting and have no updates to share. You should…

A) Nod thoughtfully and ask, "Have we considered all potential touchpoints here?"

B) Admit you don't have any updates but promise to follow up later.

C) Offer to "circle back" with details in an email.

It's the end of the day, and you're leaving your desk. To make it look like you've been busy all day, you should…

A) Leave a few sticky notes with words like "Urgent" on your monitor and scatter some pens around.

B) Keep your computer on, with an open spreadsheet and a coffee mug half-finished nearby.

C) Tidy everything up completely so your desk looks spotless.

You're caught daydreaming during a long meeting. The best recovery move is to…

A) Quickly nod and say, "That's a really interesting point!"

B) Ask a vague question like, "What metrics are we using to measure success here?"

C) Apologize for zoning out and promise to review the meeting notes later.

You're on your third coffee break of the day, and someone comments on your trips to the machine. You should…

A) Smile and say, "I'm just recharging for a big deadline I'm tackling."

B) Mention that "caffeine boosts productivity" and carry on.

C) Say, "Just a quick break—I'm on a tight deadline."

Scoring Key:
- Mostly A's: You're a budding productivity faker— well on your way to mastery but still room to add finesse.
- Mostly B's: You've perfected the art of looking busy —your responses are seamless and believable!
- Mostly C's: You're an undercover productivity expert, but don't be afraid to add a bit more flair to your tactics.

A FINAL WORD OF ENCOURAGEMENT

The ultimate office survival skill is knowing when to work hard and when to work smart. With the tips, tactics, and strategies you've now mastered, you're ready to tackle any office situation with ease and confidence.

In the end, faking productivity is an art. It's about balancing appearance with intention, showing up with purpose, and knowing when to shine (and when to blend in). Remember, there's a difference between being busy and being effective—and with these skills, you'll be both.

So go forth, Certified Office Productivity Faker, and may your days be as productive (or creatively unproductive) as you choose. Here's to mastering the art of balance, leaving just the right impression, and— most importantly—owning your time in the office.
Now... take a coffee break. You've earned it.

Made in United States
Orlando, FL
03 December 2024

54666056R00046